Sangoma's Divining Bones

Ngwanatemane Ivy Segane Mofokeng

Copyright © 2016 Ngwanatemane Ivy Segane Mofokeng

All rights reserved.

ISBN: -10: 1540896277
ISBN-13:9781540896278

DEDICATION

To all my beloved spiritual children around the world, your baba's book is your inheritance.

This book is for new initiates who never got a chance or should I rather say "luck" to learn divination through bones while they were at initiation school. Learn what is here and discover the rest through your ancestors.

CONTENTS

chapter	Acknowledgments	I
1	Four sets of divining bones	01
2	Attributes of divining bones	Pg. 02
3	When bones are alive	Pg. 03
4	When bones appear dead	Pg. 06
5	Divining bones in pictures	Pg. 11
6	Divining bone incantation	Pg. 32
7	Contact details	Pg. 33

ACKNOWLEDGMENTS

for you seeker of knowledge "watch the tortoise, he makes a progress when he sticks his neck out"

CHAPTER 1 **FOUR SETS OF DIVINING BONES**

Divining bones are classed into four sets

1. Dipetlwa (elephants)
2. Meetsi (water shells)
3. Dikhudu (tortoises)
4. Dithlako (goat-Heels)

All four sets consist of the following persons:

An adult female

An adult male

A young female

A young male

SANGOMA'S DIVINING BONES

CHAPTER 2: ATTRIBUTES OF DIVINING BONES

1. ELEPHANTS

Elephant bones generally represents:

POSITIVE TRAITS: The strength, patients, the gifts of healing, spiritual gifts, divination and wisdom

NEGATIVE TRAITS: short tempered, evil, witchcraft, arrogance, jealous, and envy

2. WATER SHELLS

A seashell in divination generally represents:

POSITIVE TRAITS: Water, love, a home, fertility, life and peace.

NEGATIVE TRAITS: death, quarrels, misery, blocked third eye, hallucination.

3 TORTOISE

A tortoise in divination generally represents:

POSITIVE TRAITS: Ancestors, gods, longevity, morals, wisdom, security, stable life, knowledge, patience

NEGATIVE TRAITS: delays, carelessness, grumpy, anxiety, irresponsible

3. GOAT

A Goat bone in divination generally represents:

POSITIVE TRAITS: Sacrifice, abundance, independence, courage, faith, wisdom, peace, and masculinity

NEGATIVE TRAITS: Fearful, clumsy, ignorant, disturbed, agitated,

SANGOMA'S DIVINING BONES

CHAPTER 3: WHEN BONES APPEAR ALIVE

When you throw the divining bones and:

The whole set of one or more (either all elephants, or all shells, or all tortoises or all bones) are alive (alive means: the part with dots, writings or numbers is visible, we call it **Mpherefere** (there are quarrels, misunderstanding, physical or spiritual fighting, war, confusion and etc. in the patient's life)

AM, YM, YF, AF

1. **MPHEREFERE**: it's simply quarrels, unrest or confusion
   When <u>an adult female</u> is the only one alive and all three are dead in one or more sets we call it:

   o O o AF

2. **MABONA** (mabona is a seer, or a spiritually active person, he see visions and meaningful dreams it can be that he is not a seer at all but he saw something that puzzled him hence he is here to consult)

When <u>an adult male</u> is the only one alive and all three bones are dead in one or more sets we call it:

AM o O O

3. **LEGWAME**: (legwame is a wise person, gifted with healing and spiritual matters, with gods of wealth, he will live long provided he answer his calling, it can also mean a very ailing person who will die soon)

It is up to the initiate to listen to his spirit to what exactly this legwame is about and tell the patient the correct information.

When <u>a young female</u> is the only one alive and all three are dead in one or more sets we call it:

o o YF o

4. **LENGWANA**: (lengwana is a person who has been fed poisonous Muthi, the stomach bloats, he will die soon, and it sometimes mean the person is wealthy or going to be extremely wealthy)

SANGOMA'S DIVINING BONES

When <u>a young male</u> is the only one alive and all three are dead in one or more sets we call it:

O ✞m O O

5. **MASESELLE** (maseselle is a person who day dreams, she/he sometimes don't know what time or day it is, this person has emotional or psychological issues, he won't be surprised to find himself undergoing mental evaluation or taking antidepressants in the near future. This person has a lot of baggage over their shoulders, they will run mad one day, they need spiritual intervention, the ancestors are not happy)

Check if it is the hand of a witch or normal day to day stress due to responsibilities overwhelming them.

<u>An adult male and a young female</u> when they are both alive we call it:

Am O YF O

6. **SETHLAKO** (sethlako means difficult journey in case of a person who is embarking on a journey either physical or spiritual, attending a job interview they might not make it, they need intervention, it advices a person to be strong and courageous, it advices a person to stop doubting themselves, that it is not the end of the world, that the road ahead is not easy but they must put their trust into their personal god, it can also mean the person had or will have a problem with sore feet, or the leg might be broken soon due to a curse put inside one of his shoes, it also means the person must take a major decision.

<u>An adult female and a young female:</u>

O O YF AF

7. **BOKGATHA** (bokgatha is female issues, it means the patient is either a victim of female enemies, or if a male his weakness is women, or women are ganging up against him and want to destroy him, it can also mean female reproductive issues, bloated tummy, menstrual problems, blood stasis, bladder, gal, cyst, fibroids, infertility, miscarriages and etc. it is up to the initiate to learn how to differentiate between this bokgatha issue regarding the patient.

SANGOMA'S DIVINING BONES

Obviously you cannot diagnose a male client with female reproductive problems??

An adult male and adult female

AM O O AF

8. **MOGOLORI** (mogolori is adults issues, witchcraft, evil, arrogance, obnoxious persons, a person who had no morals or a good heart, that person can be the same one you are conducting a reading for or his enemies, be careful here. Listen to your spirit. The client can be a victim of those kind of person or himself is the culprit.

An adult female and a young male:

O YM O AF

9. **SEPHATHAKGO** (sephathakgo means a favoured person, a chid of the gods, a gifted person, not necessarily spiritual, it can be wealth, or fame, or beauty, brains etc., the person can have a rough past, from suffering but now the gods says to him "do not worry, we have been listening to your prayers and we are about to bless you."

An adult male and young male

AM YM O O

10. **MASHUPSE**: (mashupse mean plots, jail, hexes, jinx, ties, chains, blockages, against the patient) just check well what this mashupse is all about here. Other bones will give you clue

A young male and a young female

O YM YF O

11. **THLAPADIMA**: (thlapadima means lies, deception, pretenders, backstabbers, something that appears as real but it is not, untrustworthy person) when you see the bones are thlapadima you must be very careful, because this can refer to the same person you are conducting a reading for, they might be testing you, they might be sent by witches or other spiritualists to test your abilities, they might be imposter, they might be lying about what they really want from you, but on the other hand it might be that they are a victim to lies and backstabbing. Check what

SANGOMA'S DIVINING BONES

other bones say in order to establish what exactly the issue here is. Listen to your spirit.

CHAPTER 4: WHEN BONES APPEAR DEAD

When you throw the divining bones and:

The whole set of one or more (either all elephants, or all shells, or all tortoises or all bones) dead (dead means: the part with dots, wrings or numbers is not visible)

When the part with numbers, dots or writings is hidden underneath we call it:

○ ○ ○ ○

12. **MOHLAKOLA** (Mohlakola means there is either theft of loss) it can be loss of life, pets or property even live stock.

It is up to the initiate to listen to his spirit to what exactly this Mohlakola is about and tell the patient the correct information.

When one is dead and all three are alive:

<u>When a young female is dead</u> *AMYM O AF*

13. **MAKGOLELA** (meaning a pregnant female, if it's a male client they are having issues in their tummy, if they aren't aware of it is because the Muthi is hidden to their knowledge in order to kill them slow, but the proof will be bad breath, or bloated stomach, in worse case swollen feet and kidney failure, or backache, taking days to go to toilet, darker and darker complexion, it can also mean nemesis, that they have started something now it is confusing them, they must finish what they have started, it is their own doing, it might also mean they are hallucinating or have the tendency to talk by themselves.

<u>When a young male is dead</u> *AM O YF AF*

14. MORAROMOGOLO (it means enemies are close family members) it

SANGOMA'S DIVINING BONES

doesn't matter who the enemy is, just advise them to be very careful because the enemy is closer to them, and help them to see the enemy suffering the consequences of their actions, do not reveal the names, the patient will soon realize who their enemy is after you have performed rituals on them

<u>When an adult male is dead</u>

                                    O Ym 4F AF

15. **SAMORARWANA**: (it means the enemies are blood relatives, neighbours or friends) it doesn't matter who the enemy is, just advise them to be very careful because the enemy is closer to them, and help them to see the enemy suffering the consequences of their actions, do not reveal the names, the patient will soon realise who their enemy is after you have performed rituals on them.

<u>When an adult female is dead</u>

                                   am Ym YF O

16. **MABJANA** (mabjana means quarrels, noise, mourning, madness, a nosy noisy neighbour, wife, woman or a witch) meaning the person you are divining for can be a witch or can be mad as a result of nemesis, that they have been a bad person now they are suffering the consequences, it can also mean they are mourning a death of a closed one, or their life is surrounded with madness, quarrelling and witchcraft, this one is complicated, you need to take your ancestors brew often in order to be able to conduct a divination and be able to distinguish between a witch of a client or a client who is suffering a witch, one mistake you will be trapped in their circle, you cannot help a person who is mad because of their own doings, it will affect you and you will suffer like them.

It can also mean the person is been sent by witches to test you, or to get your Muthi and use it to hit you. When Mabjana bone is facing you...be very concerned.

SANGOMA'S DIVINING BONES

EXTRA BONES

1. Crocodile
2. Impalas
3. Monkeys
4. Lions
5. Crystals
6. Domingo
7. Marula seeds
8. Crafted sticks
9. Ndindili (gogo)
10. dice

ANCESTORS:

1. Two Wild pig bones
2. One Sambane bone

I personally use only monkeys, dice, Ndindili, crystals and black Domingo as extras.

Red crystal stone is used to look at the blood of the patient, to find out if they will live long or not, if they are suffering from blood diseases or immune deficiency. The red crystal alone cannot conclude that the person is suffering from blood related issues. You need further examination from other bones.

Red crystal can also mean that the person has what we call Isiqhitho in Zulu (bad blood) meaning they have bad luck as a result of a curse, either from human waste Muthi, millipede, dead black dog maggots, dog poo, sewage water, corps water and all those type of bad blood curses made by witches.

Royal Blue one represent the blue genie, the goddess or Nzunza (mermaid)

SANGOMA'S DIVINING BONES

White stone represent the Christian angels (isithunywa)

Transparent stone represent water (marine) spirits

The wild pigs represent the divining, healing, Nguni, ndau and Sangoma ancestors

The Sambane bone represent the general family ancestors.

To find out what type of ancestors one has we look at the black sea stone, the royal blue stone, the white stone, the transparent stone, the wild pigs and Sambane.

When **Sambane** is alive during divination it means the problem is within the family ancestors, they either want appeasing as soon as possible, or they have a complain regarding some issues, maybe the family is quarrelling too much and the ancestors aren't happy, or someone is a drunkard and it makes them concerned, or any other issue that doesn't sit well with them. It is up to you to find out why are the ancestors up against the person, or have turned against the person.

We say the ancestors have turned against you when they appear facing you, an ancestor must not face you, an ancestor must lead the way and you come from behind, if they come from the front then there is a huge problem.

As a spiritualist if you perform a divination on someone you must first look at the ancestors before any other thing, they must not face you or face the client.

If they face you then you are in deep shit. When the client is gone do self-divination and see what went wrong between you and them and fix it as soon as possible.

The black stone from the sea represent royalty, if the person is from royal bloodline they will sometimes also have mermaid or goddess spirit. The stones are meaningful only when they appear alive during

SANGOMA'S DIVINING BONES

divination.

Not everyone is given this stone to use for divination, and you cannot find it at the Muthi market or store, only at the sea where they will sent you to go pick one or two.

It is said that in the old days, the worriers, chiefs and kings used to swallow the stone in order to have supernatural powers. I was given three and I swallowed one, and have two remaining for divination, one represent a god and one a goddess. That is how I see when one is a monarch.

Let me stress that if you are a monarch Sangoma, you will always attract monarchy clients, because they are sent to you by their gods.

Do not worry this book is not for morchs it is for every spiritualist who wish to learn bone reading and divination

SANGOMA'S DIVINING BONES

CHAPTER 5: DIVINING BONES IN PICTURES

This white stone represent angels or a gift of heavenly (messengers of any religion), in a Christian way we call it isithunywa gift.

SANGOMA'S DIVINING BONES

This **red stone** one we use to read the blood of a client, the position it is appearing with means the client has not bad blood, or any serious illness.

When it is facing down it mean there is a serious health problem with your client. It normally is related to blood issues like hypertension, sugar diabetes, HIV, cancer, TB and all other immune deficiency problems. Work together with the health officials here.

It can also be bad blood as a result of hexes or generation to generation curses.

SANGOMA'S DIVINING BONES

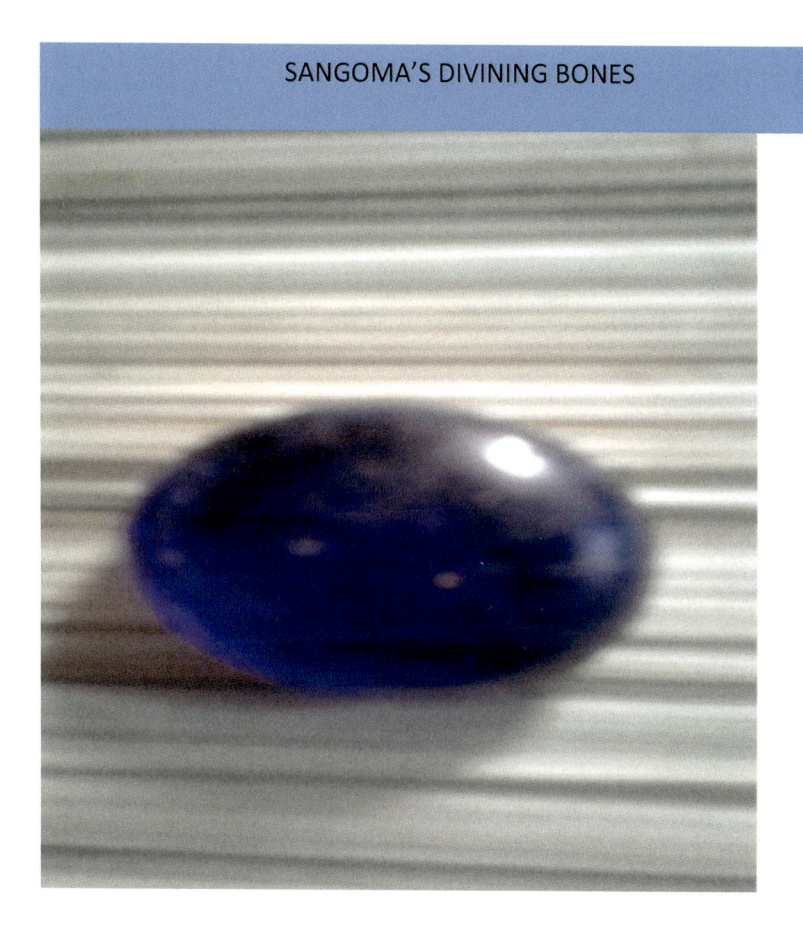

The **royal blue** stone represent the mermaid or Nzunza spirit for a novice Sangoma, an experienced Sangoma doesn't need this stone to read a person with Nzunza gift, they will sense them immediately when they enter the shrine. They come with cold breeze or rain, and they also normally have wet hands or feet

You will also see one or all of their eye, there is a mark or signs in there. This you must learn on your own. It is said that baloyi ba tsebana ka lehlaka (witches recognize each other by a mark, if you are not a mermaid you will not know one)

When the blue stone appears in the position it is in right now, it means the person is gifted with Nzunza spirit.

They suffer water dreams or visions, the water in a dream are violent or always chasing them. They see marine people in their dream.

SANGOMA'S DIVINING BONES

A mermaid stone is one, it is not necessary to have male and female stones to ascertain whether the client has a merman or mermaid, in my experience a mermaid goes together with a merman because even if your mermaid is still single in the spiritual world it will eventually get married one day. And she/ He will introduce you to her Husband/ wife. You will be the second wife or husband to the mermaid/man. Thats how far as the marine world or life goes when coming to ancestral calling. You are a lover of a mermaid/man if you are called by them.

Today we are talking about divination not mermaids so I will not go further than this.

This transparent stone is used to read a person with a general water spirit gift. The gift can be used for prophesy or divination as a healer. Water spirit gift is not a mermaid or Nzunza spirit, it simply is a gift of

SANGOMA'S DIVINING BONES

ancestors who resides inside the oceans or any huge river. Other ancestors stay in mountains or wilderness, but this ones stay specifically inside the water.

When a person is initiated under ancestors who resides in waters, they must take an ancestors brew prepared with river, lake or spring water.

They must venerate their ancestors in a river not in a mountain or cave, unless otherwise there is a well or spring inside that cave.

It only have a meaning when it is appearing it the above position or form, if it is facing upside down it doesn't have any meaning, meaning the client doesn't have any water gifts.

A person with water spirit gifts also suffers violent water dreams. The difference is they see normal ancestors in their dreams, others see snakes. They don't see mermaids in their dreams and their gifts and attributes differs from those of mermaid gifted persons.

Mind you: in case of a mermaid gifted person both the transparent and royal blue stones must be active in order to divine that they are called by Nzunza.

SANGOMA'S DIVINING BONES

This bones represent ancestors, they are bones from wild pigs. The big one represent the Nguni ancestors, the small one represent ndau ancestors.

We don't have male or female ancestors in this bones because in the beginning healers were male only. For us to find out if the ancestor in you is male or female we need to ask questions or dig deeper into the spirit world to find answers. Anyway it is not necessary to learn whether the spirits are male or female, the client will eventually know once they start initiation. It will definitely be revealed. Anyway almost all of us somehow have both male and female ancestor in them. So gender is not necessary.

SANGOMA'S DIVINING BONES

This are ordinary goats' bones, taken from the initiate's goats, you cannot buy these bones from the Muthi market or shops, they are taken out of the goats an initiate used while undergoing initiation. From each goat slaughtered there are two bones that are removed from their heels. That's why we call this bones "heels" (Dithlako)

SANGOMA'S DIVINING BONES

This is MOHLAKOLA. This type of Mohlakola is read from Domingos, Mohlakola from this type of bones means there is a black cloud hanging over the client's life, it also means death, the client can be mourning death in their family, may be that is why they are here, to find out what took away the life of their loved one, or what really happened during their death.

You should dig deeper to find out what does this type of Mohlakola really mean to the client.

But most definitely its about death, just find out who died, how did they die and etc.

SANGOMA'S DIVINING BONES

This Elephant bones/ white Mohlakola means loss of property due to theft, or loss of livestock, loss of memory or even a missing person. If you have black Domingos in your divining bag and this type of Mohlakola appears (elephant) you should know that there is no way that is can be death, unless if your ancestors don't allow you to use black Domingos and you have only the elephant bones then you will have to dig deeper into the spirit world to ascertain whether this Mohlakola is about death or theft.

Because an elephant represent strength and energy it also mean that the client does not have strength or energy anymore due to the incident that has just happened recently. Domingos are used to ascertain death when they are in a Mohlakola state. Elephant Mohlakola represent stolen power in a form of physical or spiritual gifts.

SANGOMA'S DIVINING BONES

This above two bones are made from an elephant, here they are alive. We say they are alive because the dots are showing, the above four bones before this two represent Mohlakola, and they are dead because the dots are underneath.

This two bones represent women, they are women because of their shape, they have a V shape at the bottom, that is how we differentiate them from males. It is not necessary to go and look for the exact shapes, you can differentiate yours by the number of dots if you cannot find the

SANGOMA'S DIVINING BONES

V-shaped ones. If you only get all flat at the bottom, you should mark them by their number of dots, say may be the ones with many dots are males and the ones with few dots are females vice versa, do not worry, the ancestors are listening while you announce that. They will not let you down and confuse you while you perform your divination.

Just do not go back on your decision as to which one is male which one is female.

If it is difficult to get used to the bones through the number of dots then find yourself a sharp instrument and make a V-shape at the bottom of the chosen female, remember that one female must be big and the other one be small, same as males.

Here we have a young female and an adult female. The adult female has many dots, the young female has few dots.

When two females are alive we call the divination "BOKGATHA". Female issues.

Women are powerful and determined type of human beings. When you see two women looking at each other and whispering, you should know that whatever they are planning or plotting will come to pass.

They don't easily go back on their plans. When you do divination and two women are appearing, know that whatever that you are about to find out its very serious and you must advice the client to act fast.

An elephant remembers everything, therefore Bokgatha from elephant bones must not be taken lightly. An elephant is patient, calm and very conscious.

If your client is in a legal fight with another person and the bones come out an elephant Bokgatha, it means that the other person is powerful than your client, the person will stop at nothing, he is patient, he doesn't mind waiting for the results for a long time, even if your client was dragging their feet to meet a mutual agreement with them, they

SANGOMA'S DIVINING BONES

will be patient while fighting tooth and nail to see best results for themselves.

The above is a Dice, it's one of the extras we add to our divining bones, two dices are enough, the one with six numbers represent family member. Issues arise from a family of the client. Enemies are from within. Problems arise from within, or any other matters are from within. It is up to you to ascertain what exactly is this family member

SANGOMA'S DIVINING BONES

doing to the poor client.

This two dices one represent a car one represent a hex. The one with four dots is a car, either a previous car accident or a future one, it can also mean the client should be driving their own car but they still travelling by public transport due to some issues or bad luck or whatever that you may find during divination. It might also mean the client has issues whit their car, it can be due to the car being a victim of tikoloshi that keep breaking the car parts or something. It is up to you to dig deeper. The bones are there to guide you or give you a clue, they don't conclude the whole process. You need to get serious in connecting with the spirits.

The **dice with five numbers** represent a hex or cross. The client is being hexed, nothing good is moving for them, someone has made a covenant against them, or someone has sworn against them. Whatever it is that an enemy or a witch has done on them it must be removed because nothing good will happen to this client and his next generations.

SANGOMA'S DIVINING BONES

The **dice with one number** represent a knot, a spiritual knot. Or tie. It means the client is being curse with either a knot made from their own hair or clothes, or a rope, a wool or piece of string, plant root, part of a plant, wire or a cloth and etc.

The **dice with two dots** represent a seer (MABONA) mabona means a person who can see through a third eye, or it can be that your client has seen a strange thing hence he decided to come ask for divination. Do not do a guess work, tell the client exactly what do they see, do they see visions or they see a strange thing and it made them decide to consult you?

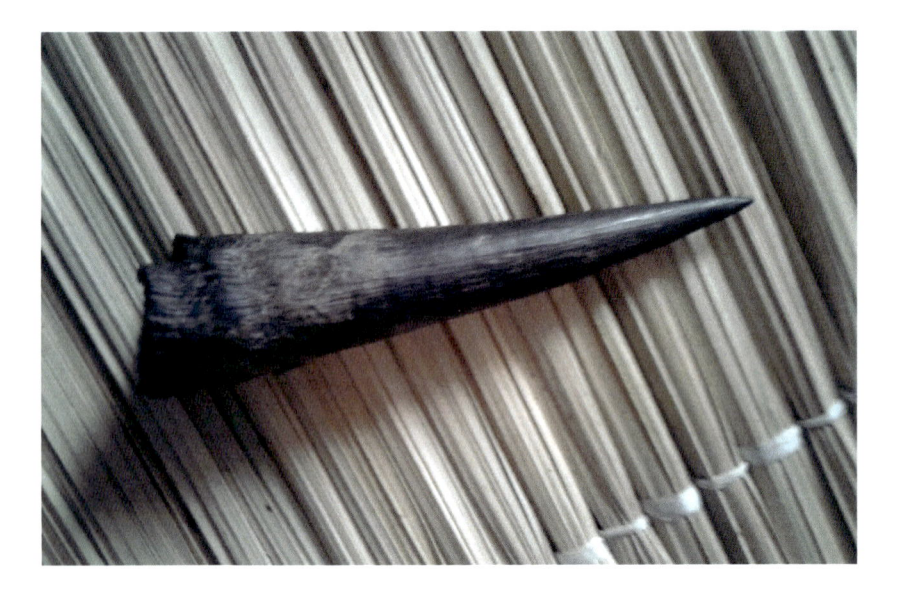

This horn is an additional item for divination, it represents a weapon. It can be spiritual or physical weapon. It only communicates when it is facing a bone that represent the client, or it is directly facing the position where the client is sitting. This client need protection from spiritual or physical attacks.

It might also mean that this client is suffering sharp stabbing pains somewhere in their body. Dig deeper, that's your duty to find out where

SANGOMA'S DIVINING BONES

exactly are they feeling the pains. It is also your duty to remove those pains if they request a healing ritual from you.

Look at the above bones closely, they differ from the female elephant bones that represents BOKGATHA. This bones represent a young and an adult male. They are referred to as MASHUPSE.

They are not V-shaped like the previous ones, they are flat at the bottom because they represent males.

Mashupse generally means jail, hex, crossing, jinx, ties, backstabbing and all those type of things. When MASHUPHSE appears in a form of an

SANGOMA'S DIVINING BONES

elephant it means the witch is tying or hexing your client's strength, patience, gifts of healing, spiritual gifts, divination and wisdom. They simply are against their shaman power.

The above bones are made from Tortoise. A tortoise represent longevity, wealth, wisdom, a traveler or explorer, sometimes a tramp, because anywhere they wish to sleep they do.

The above picture represent MPHEREFERE. Remember Mpherefere is quarrelling, misunderstanding, spiritual wars or attacks and etc.? MPHEREFERE in a tortoise form is not good because it means there is war against a client regarding either wealth, hidden treasures, spiritual gifts, wisdom or health. This person might end up roaming around the streets with no real place to stay. May be they are fighting for a house or any valuables left behind by their parents?

It also means whoever is fighting them is targeting at their gifts. They want to take them away or block them.

Advice the patient to avoid quarrels because the enemies are engineering them on purpose in order to get what they want. Perform a protection ritual on them.

This is the opposite of MOHLAKOLA. This is what we call MPHEREFERE. This one is appearing in an elephant form. Mpherefere of this type is taking away the power, focus, patience and spiritual gifts of the client.

If they entertain this quarrels and fights they will end up losing focus and patience. They will jump from one religion or belief to another. In a long run they will go around losing their spiritual gifts to different pastors, healer and prophets.

SANGOMA'S DIVINING BONES

Advice the client to stay in a peaceful and calm place surrounded by loving persons.

MPHERE FERE appearing in Domingos. This type of Mpherefere is dangerous because the opposite of it is death. When those dots are underneath it's a death Mohlakola. It means this type of quarrelling is aiming at killing the client. Advice a client to ignore this quarrels, they must try and iron out the confusion and misunderstandings. You need to perform a protection spell on them. If possible they must avoid the persons who are initiating the quarrels. A spell was casted on purpose to make the client attract quarrel and misunderstanding into their life.

SANGOMA'S DIVINING BONES

 Stone for monarchs. This is an extra. Don't worry if you don't have it. It is given to certain individuals.

You can have it but if your ancestors were not royal persons or advisors to royal persons it might be very strong for them and make divination difficult for you. It can curse your bag. I personally do not have an extra stone to sell or giveaway. But if the gods instruct me to find one for you I will definitely do.

SANGOMA'S DIVINING BONES

<u>Young and adult males</u>

When a young and adult male are alive we call it **MASHUPSE**

This is a sea Shell **MASHUPSE.**

The client who bones appear in a form of sea shell mashupse is a victim of crossing or tying of: marine powers, love, a home, fertility, life and peace.

This person will lose the spiritual gift from either mermaids or family ancestors who resides inside the waters. Their love life is not going well, there is no peace at home, life is not easy and there is no peace in their life. In short their life is being tied inside a witch's bottle or buried somewhere between the boulders.

Dig deeper and find out what exactly is going on here.

SANGOMA'S DIVINING BONES

This is **BOKGATHA** appearing in a form of seashells. Bokgatha mean issues with women or women issues.

If your client is a woman first look at women issues like fertility, menstrual problems, blood stasis and etc.

If it is issues with women then look at things like: women enemies plotting to steal marine powers, trying to steal a lover, disturbing peace, or plotting to get the client removed from work or their home.

If it's a male you should also look at issues related to sexual dysfunction, poor erection, early ejaculation, bad temper, mood swings and etc.

SANGOMA'S DIVINING BONES

CHAPTER 6: DIVINING BONE INCANTATIONS: DIRETO TJA DITAOLA

My people use poems to better understand the bones. It is unfortunate that I will not write this poems in English.

1 MPHEREFERE

Ga selematsela go tsogile kgang ya letjatji, malatjie le malatjana baalwa, mongwe ore letjatji letjwa ka bodibeng, mongwe ore letjwa phagong ya morula, kgang etlo lala lemang naa, kgang etlo lala le malatjana gobane ele ngwane monnyane.

2 THLAPADIMA

Ke thlapadima yaleme lemaka tjibogo labakwena bakgaga baile kalona bare tjibogo le a lena kubu a lena kwena alena selumi semetseng (LIES)

3 SETHLAKO

Ke sethlako sa monna mosepedi, sethlako sa ramatlema bare tlema sethlako setiye oseke waba mokgokolo mothisha leeto, tsela tja boroka ketje thata dikgona ke batho ba go namela dithaba. (determination needed)

4 MAKGOLELA

Diwele makgolela, bare lekgolela kela phahlana geele tlou eshitwa ke mmogo. (Victim of own circumstance)

5. MASHUPJE

Ke mashupje a bashimane ba Malala kgotla 'moraka, bashimane bago reile ka dipala monwana tja maoto letja matsogo. (Victim of their own maids)

SANGOMA'S DIVINING BONES

6 BOKGATHA
Ke bokgatha bongaangaa roko jwa pudi botjwa thlakong, oseka wabona naka tja pudi goratana go bapelana gare tjona gonale bokgatha! (Enemies are women who are very close to each other)

7 MOHLAKOLA
Matsepe o hlakotje mogatja kgoshi ditjwaro ka moshate a shala a ponapona (theft/loss)

8. MORARO MOGOLO
Ke moraro mogolo wa sedikodiko nthethelegwa motse, le ora mahlaku le aketja balata, geele mahlaku ona le or aka noshi (victim of your own blood/ relatives)

9. SAMORARWANA
Samorarwana a se kgole sekgatha nko le molomo nkase bitja seka nkaraba. (Enemies are not far from you/close relatives, friends, colleagues or neighbours)

10 LEGWAME
La moriri moshweu seala sa hlolo bahu ba hwile ba olla. (Wealth/wisdom)

11 MABONA
A mma kasa ka bona ka tloga kese mmoni ke nnoshi geele gobona gona retla bona (spiritual gifted/saw a strange thing and decided to visit a seer)

12 LENGWANA
La mafa kudu oseka ware gofa ngwana marega kappa selemo wa mollela tlala ware o khoshe goba ona tlala. (Abundance / food poisoning)

SANGOMA'S DIVINING BONES

13 MASESELLE
Wa sesella moopa, geele ngwana gaa seselle (a hallucinating person, a barren woman)

14 SEPHATHAKGO
Sa mmahlatji a boroka sa nkwana checheche, chipa namela mooka mabala a shaletje mookeng wena kgwadi ya mabala osa utame gobane okwetje. (The gods has heard your prayers/ a blessed person)

15 MOGOLORI
E mogolo mokaka tlou, gake mogolo moja sa motho ke mogolo moja saka, monyane gea sena mogolo ga ke moje kea morathaganya. (A witch/ arrogant person)

16. MABJANA
A leshata leshagashaga molapo, mosadi wa leshata omo agele motse thabeng leshata le tjee ka molapo wa thaba (quarrels /misunderstandings)

Contact details:
Facebook: torchofthegods Segane Mofokeng
Email: ivy.mofokeng3@gmail.com
Mobile: 27720883995
Blog: madlozimuthi.blogspot.com
Google+: gogo Shlahla

May the great gods delight your heart…

Made in the
USA
Columbia, SC